GW01005381

WHOLE TRUTH OR HALF TRUTH

Is there a right answer?

Enjoy reading the real-life examples to find out.

Petrina Ten FCCA FCA

WHOLE TRUTH OR HALF TRUTH

© 2020 Petrina Ten

ISBN : 9798652361143

Every effort has been made to trace copyright holders and obtain their permission for the use of copyright material.

Every effort has been made to give credit to the relevant persons who have created the quotations used in this book.

A BIG THANK YOU TO :

My family, especially Ronald, Helen, Kenneth, Ann, Jarrett, Aunty Vivienne, Aunty Anita and Uncle Richard and my circle of friends who have supported me throughout the years.

My nephew Ryan who has been ever so patient with me and helped in editing and formatting this book.

Richard and Anne Glynne-Jones for being one of the first couples to take such great care of me when I first arrived in London on my own almost 30 years ago.

All Mentors who have encouraged and taught me so much more about how to manage the challenging journey called life and to appreciate every moment. **Chapter 22 is dedicated to all of you.**

James Nicholson, Jessen James, Chloë Bisson, Dea Fileva, Fabio Errante and Tanya Grant for your continued guidance on best paths to follow.

Darren-Lee Joseph for your continued support as I continue to document more of my knowledge and experiences.

Everyone else that has touched and influenced my journey, there are far too many to name individually, you know who you are. We have met for a special reason.

All our followers of Planet Wellness and Super Health Food Recipes Facebook pages, subscribers of our Planet Wellness Youtube channel, thank you for your continued support and trust in our guidance.

Finally, thank you to all readers for investing your time to read this book, my first of many more to be published. I look forward to connecting with each one of you soon.

Please feel free to connect with me on
calendly.com/wellnessiridology

DEFINITION OF STUPID :

Knowing the Truth
Seeing the Truth,
but still believing the Lies.

WHOLE TRUTH OR HALF TRUTH

PREFACE

This book is dedicated to my last surviving grandmother, Barbara, my mother's mother who passed away peacefully in August 2013. Despite not going to College or University, she did a lot of reading and often spoke her mind whenever I visited her. It is also dedicated to my beloved dad, Yen Wee, who passed away peacefully in November 2018.

WHAT INSPIRED THIS BOOK?

It is my dear, forever active, although long retired mother, Helen who was feeling bored after completing a personal book on our family. She casually asked me one day in December several years ago for some ideas on what her next book should be on. Having just gone through and putting up with all the usual end of year festivities and the hypocrisies that normally come with it, I casually replied 'How about a book on all the half-truths people tell all year round?' To my surprise, she responded, 'Good idea' and so here we are!

ABOUT THIS BOOK

Whilst this book contains real life events and examples, which I hope friends and relatives will enjoy reminiscing on and readers can relate to, it has not been written with any intention to offend the sensitive. It is just a truthful and hopefully humorous way of looking at life, as it has occurred from my perspective.

As William Shakespeare wrote in his play,

AS YOU LIKE IT – *"All the world's a stage and all the men and women merely players"*.

We have all been brought up to be actors and actresses of some sorts to survive in this world. Just like everyone else, I too have been guilty of telling some half-truths in my lifetime for the sake of maintaining some level of diplomacy. Despite this, I still believe that honesty is still the best policy. It is easier said than done though. The truth may hurt but if one is mentally mature enough to accept it, the Whole Truth is always better than Half-Truth.

Always tell the truth.
If you cannot always tell the truth, do not lie.

1

PLEASE SIR, CAN I HAVE SOME MORE?
Charles Dickens' play Oliver Twist

I have lived half my life in Malaysia and half of it in the United Kingdom. It is therefore easier for me to make comparisons and understand different cultures.

In Malaysia, we are brought up to turn down offers of second helpings with meals until the host asks and keeps inviting you several times to change your mind. We were taught that this is the 'Malaysian' thing to do; the polite way of not showing one is greedy.

When I first visited England and was fortunate enough to be welcome at several of my parents' English friends' homes, I was warned that the British literally took 'yes' as 'yes' and 'no' as 'no'. They will not ask twice to check if you changed your mind after giving the initial answer. Unfortunately, due to the upbringing that was instilled in me for twenty years, old habits and traditions die hard. I of course enjoyed the hosts' home cooking and wanted seconds on some courses.

However, the 'Malaysian' in me answered 'no thanks' when asked and I was not offered a second chance. Okay, that made me learn fast re the differences between East and West but as I say, most of us are merely greedy most of the time and of course I did not die of hunger or malnutrition on such occasions. I just learnt to say 'yes, please' if I wanted more in future. In this case, the whole truth would have pleased the host and the guest's cravings for second helpings too!

Honesty is the rarest wealth anyone can possess, and yet all the honesty in the world ain't lawful tender for a loaf of bread. - Josh Billings

PERSONAL NOTES

Describe a similar situation in your life :

_____

_____

_____

_____

_____

Describe how you may now choose to act differently :

_____

_____

_____

_____

_____

2

HONESTY PAYS-LEARN FROM CHILDREN

Children are honest and say what they mean. In this context, several years ago, my elder nephew, Jarrett, age 6 at that time, enjoyed a special porridge cooked by grand aunt during the Chinese New Year celebrations.

After a mouthful of the porridge, Jarrett exclaimed, "This is what I like...yummy!" of course grand aunt was pleased that he really enjoyed her porridge.

When Jarrett returned home, he told his maternal grandmother what ingredients to put in the porridge. He was honest to tell his grandmother that he preferred this special porridge to the one that was served at home. He told the truth about his preference and his grandmother learnt how to cook this porridge and everyone at home too enjoyed the new dish.

In this scenario, telling the whole truth pays and everyone benefitted from Jarrett's honesty.

If you tell the truth you
do not have to remember anything.
- Mark Twain

PERSONAL NOTES

Describe a similar situation in your life :

_____

_____

_____

_____

_____

Describe how you may now choose to act differently :

_____

_____

_____

_____

_____

3

HONESTY PAYS-MY PERSONAL EXAMPLES

Healthier options

I enjoy chilli paste that goes very well with other foods and know a few friends who are kind enough to occasionally make this for me. They used to make it the traditional way with lots of vegetable or other oils, which are not so healthy although it is very tasty.

I was truthful in giving my friends my feedback and requested that they please just add a bit of extra virgin olive oil instead. They listened and have agreed that the improved recipe is a lot healthier and still as tasty too.

A lie may take care of the present, but it has no future.

Being honest whilst respecting various customs

In Western countries, the host will ask whether the guests would like a drink of tea or coffee. Then the preferred drink will be served accordingly, i.e. whether with milk, how much sugar, etc.

In Malaysia, most hosts will just serve the drinks without asking the guests for their preference most of the time. Nowadays, some hosts will ask the guest first their preference.

From my experience, to save myself the agony of having to drink the extremely sweet drink, be it coffee, tea, or juice, I politely ask for water or green tea. This will save me having to tell the half-truth that the drink is just right to my taste and force myself to drink it.

Nowadays we do get hosts who will ask you first your preference. But from my experience, you may still have the problem of having to drink it to be polite. Most Malay and Indian hosts often serve drinks very, very sweet, be it tea, coffee, or juice I have learnt to politely ask for water or green tea. The comment from most hosts will be, "Wow... very health conscious!" My truthful reply will be, "Yes! have to be as we grow older". So, both host and guest are happy, and no one is offended.

It is funny how everybody considers honesty a virtue, yet no one wants to hear the truth.

PERSONAL NOTES

Describe a similar situation in your life :

_____

_____

_____

_____

_____

Describe how you may now choose to act differently :

_____

_____

_____

_____

_____

4

BEING BLUNT!

This should be exercised with extreme caution; otherwise it may psychologically scar the recipient for life. In hindsight it did not scar me for life, but I was quite annoyed at the time.

My dear brother, Kenneth did this to me on at least two occasions when we were growing up and despite my forgiving him since, such words are hard to forget. What a good way to get back at him by sharing this in my book!

It was the eve of my theory driving test and being a girl, I never received a lot of moral support from my parents, where driving was concerned. My parents are overprotective and preferred that I did not pass my driving test so soon so that they could continue driving me everywhere. Being a teenager and striving for my own independence, I was of course determined to pass first time and as soon as I could. When my brother saw me doing my final revision on the eve of my examinations, he used his innocent charm to encourage me further by saying bluntly something along these lines 'You better pass this test first time as it is relatively easy and very few people fail. If you fail, you will be a real embarrassment to the family!'

There you go the whole truth as bluntly as one can put it, but it achieved results and I passed the examinations on my first attempt.

After my Form 5 (also known as GCSE or O levels in other countries), I wanted to follow the rest of my schoolmates and carry on another two years to study Form 6 (also known as A levels or NVQ Level 3 in other countries) in the local schools.

My parents could not afford to send me overseas at the time and going to a private college to do my A levels would mean saying goodbye to my school friends, having to make new friends and also incurring extra expenses of fees.

Why would someone who lives in a warm country that has so much access to fresh food like Malaysia want to leave to study overseas, I am often asked.

As wonderful as Malaysia is, there is sadly a discriminatory system, amongst those who are classed as non Bumiputera (native). Despite being born in Malaysia and being a Malaysian Citizen, my Chinese ancestry classes my family as non-native. This means there is a huge lifetime discrimination, be it in education or working life.

My brother who had gone through Form 6 and achieved very good grades did not want me to suffer the same fate as he had. The biased education system in Malaysia did not allocate adequate places in local Universities to do the Degree of your choice unless you are of a specific race and classed as a native.

My brother's grades were not good enough to be offered a place at the local Universities. However, his grades were so great that he was awarded scholarships to study in Universities in Singapore and Ireland where there were no such discriminations.

Once again, my brother could have put this tactfully but thought it would be more effective being blunt. His words to me were something along these lines 'Academically at this stage you are dumber than I am, so do not waste your time in Form 6 as you will not stand a chance getting a place in the local Universities if I did not make it with my good grades!'

The whole truth again as bluntly as one's sibling can put it.

**The truth may hurt for a little while,
but a lie hurts forever.**

PERSONAL NOTES

Describe a similar situation in your life :

_____

_____

_____

_____

_____

Describe how you may now choose to act differently :

_____

_____

_____

_____

_____

5

TV ADDICTS

For the past few years, since rekindling long lost friendships established since primary and secondary school days, a group of us make an effort to meet up for a meal several times a year despite our ever hectic personal and working lives.

On one occasion, some of us met up, had a good meal and chat, and had planned to visit another friend nearby who could not join us earlier. Unfortunately, we were running late, and the finals of the addictive reality shows, X Factor and Strictly Come Dancing were on later that night. Most of us had at least over an hour's commute before getting home and visiting this friend would mean we would have to watch the show at the friend's home and it would be really late for all of us ladies to commute home alone afterwards.

We could have told this friend a half truth. However, as we had known each other since school days, I am glad all of us were brave enough to be frank and just admitted we wanted to get home in time to watch the TV programmes live instead of watching a recording/replay. This friend was mature enough to understand and I am glad our friendship is strong enough to survive moments when we dare to tell each other the whole truth.

Nothing is better than listening to a lie
when you already know the truth.

My nephew, Ryan, when he was also about 6 years old did not want to go out with the whole family for lunch. He wanted to watch his favourite TV programme. Even at that young age, see how quickly young minds work as Ryan told a half truth.

If you know Ryan, he can never sit still. He is ever so active and always on the move. Believe me, he does not walk, but he either skips, runs, slides, swings, crawls, or hops about. We always tease him that is the reason he is so slim.

The reason Ryan gave for not wanting to go out for lunch was that he needed to lie down quietly to conserve his energy and watch TV so that he can put on some weight.

Unfortunately for Ryan, no one bought his story although it was a good attempt for a young child. We coaxed him and softened his disappointment by telling him that eating lunch will help him put on weight faster. Ryan did not kick up a fuss and obediently joined us for lunch.

PERSONAL NOTES

Describe a similar situation in your life :

_____

_____

_____

_____

_____

Describe how you may now choose to act differently :

_____

_____

_____

_____

_____

6

PUNCTUALITY

The British are renowned for this. If you turn up late at the movies, theatre, or other paid events, you may not be allowed in until interval time so that those already present are not unfairly interrupted by your lateness.

Malaysians however have a big problem with this and most often turn up late. If the appointment is at 7pm, this really means see you after 7.30pm. If the guest/attendee is polite enough, you may receive an apology for lateness; otherwise just accept it as part of the culture.

I understand we are all human and there are sometimes, genuine circumstances beyond our control that prevent us from arriving on time, such as bad weather, unexpected traffic or a personal problem that happens whilst we are on our way.

However, some people constantly use these as excuses every time. These people constantly tell half-truths and refuse to just admit they are late because they are disorganised. It is always other circumstances beyond their control and never ever their fault. Most of these people have the habit of saying something like 'I am on my way' or 'we are nearly there' when they are still hours from expected arrival time.

Majority waiting for such persons to arrive would appreciate being informed of the delay and new expected arrival time so that they can start or carry on with other tasks whilst waiting or even fit another short appointment or errand in between. This is important as we are all 'time poor' these days and time wasted is something no one can ever get back.

When I was working full time, some male relatives and friends of the Boss often took liberties by regularly arriving to work late and leaving early. They felt guilty as they had to pass my work area in the process and knew I was aware of the liberties they were taking.

The Boss was unaware of what they were up to as he was regularly away from the office. I never brought this up as I knew the Boss would always side his relatives and friends, despite knowing me a lot better and longer. One day, the guilt got the better of them and one such colleague decided to report me, saying I was constantly harassing him by looking at my watch whenever he passed by my work area. I was called to the Board Room to explain my actions.

My response? I calmly showed my wrists to the Boss and that colleague, proving I was not wearing a watch and had not worn a watch for many years. Both men were gobsmacked and as expected, never apologised for their false accusations against me. However, the truth prevailed.

Men occasionally stumble over the truth, but most of them pick themselves up and hurry off as if nothing had happened. - Winston Churchill

PERSONAL NOTES

Describe a similar situation in your life :

_____

_____

_____

_____

_____

Describe how you may now choose to act differently :

_____

_____

_____

_____

_____

7

INNOCENCE

Most of us adore children because they say and do the funniest things. Such things are only because of their innocence and ability to tell the whole truth, before the world moulds them otherwise into half-truth telling adults.

My nephew, Jarrett, age 10 at that time, went with his classmates for a camping trip. Since it was his first camping trip, he was excited over the thrill of sleeping in a tent. When his parents asked him about the trip, he said he had a wonderful time with his friends. Then he confessed that he refused to take his bath while at the camp. The reason being the bathroom was dirty and the water was cold. At least Jarrett was honest about his first camping trip.

Pretty much all the truth telling in the world is done by children. - Oliver Wendell

If you want to know the real facts, ask the child not the parent or adult they are with.

Some parents are very wary of leaving their children unattended, even with family members for fear that they may share some 'secrets' the parents do not wish other family members to be aware of.

Children are honest initially until they are introduced to fear. Fear as to what the consequences may be if the whole truth was told about their actions or non-actions. This is the stage where children start telling half-truths or none of the truth at all. When a child has say eaten the extra piece of chocolate when he or she was told not to, adults would normally scold the child for disobeying. Depending on how the situation was handled the first time, the child then slowly over time decides whether he or she should tell the whole truth or half-truth when the next 'sin' is committed.

It takes two to lie. One to lie and one to listen.
- "Homer Simpson," from the television show
The Simpsons

Has mummy become fat or ugly?

No, the daddy or adult rushes to answer before the children say anything negative for they know a few half-truths would really save the day and future from a woman who could quickly turn from Angel to Witch if the whole truth was said.

Beauty is in the eye of the beholder. There is inner and outer beauty. However, the world we live in has moulded us to give priority to outer beauty and as a result many half-truths are told.

**If you do not want to hear the truth,
do not ask the question.**

PERSONAL NOTES

Describe a similar situation in your life :

_____

_____

_____

_____

_____

Describe how you may now choose to act differently :

_____

_____

_____

_____

_____

8

DOCTOR, AM I GOING TO DIE?

This is the question often asked by a patient diagnosed with a terminal illness. It is an extremely difficult question for Doctors.

This is the stage where the unfortunate patient has often forgotten that all of us are destined to die someday. No one knows how much time each person has. The Doctor's medical knowledge and experience is normally accurate as to how much time a patient has. However, we have all read or heard real life stories where the patient has proved the Doctor's predictions wrong.

No one, however qualified or experienced can predict accurately, how long anyone has to live in this world. It is difficult to decide whether the whole truth or half-truth should be shared in this case. If the patient is a young child or mentally immature person, Doctors, family, and friends would probably choose the half-truth. The whole truth may cause the patient to go into further depression and shorten the patient's remaining lifespan and quality of their last days.

However, if the patient can handle the whole truth, this would be the preferred option. Most dying patients would then list tasks and goals that are important and prioritise how their final years, months, weeks, days, hours, and seconds could be lived. Loved ones will then have sufficient notice and make the time to say their farewells.

For those with stronger and more positive mindsets, knowing the Whole Truth may prompt the person to fight back and prove the Doctor's predictions wrong.

Truth fears no questions.

People can handle the truth,
especially when delivered with kindness.
- Libby Gill

PERSONAL NOTES

Describe a similar situation in your life :

_____

_____

_____

_____

_____

Describe how you may now choose to act differently :

_____

_____

_____

_____

_____

9

SALESPERSONS

This is probably one of the most frowned upon professions in the world.

A salesperson's main goal is to sell as they will be receiving commission on every sale, which is their livelihood. Whilst most only think that salespersons consist of those in retail, insurance, or estate agents, all of us are salespersons whether we or the world at large recognises this.

This is part of our human nature as soon as we are born. Babies communicate by crying to attract the adult's attention. When children do not get what they want, they often cry or show tantrums. This is because they have learnt from the moment they were born that this is the best way to receive the item or attention they want, especially when the adult does not initially allow them to but often give in if the child does a really good job crying.

By crying or showing tantrums, children often convince the adult that the item or attention they wanted needs to be given to them. How different is this from what salespersons do in their jobs? The salesperson's main task is to convince the prospective buyer that the item they are trying to sell is required by them.

Accountants must convince prospective clients that they are able to provide the services required, much better than their competitors and for better value for money. They must then present their clients' financial statements in the best way to please the expectations of both creditors and shareholders. It is funny as these same clients would prefer not to show such a huge taxable profit when it comes to declaring any personal or corporation tax.

Those providing education must convince parents and prospective students likewise that their establishment or service is better than those of their competitors.

There will always be a lawyer, solicitor, and barrister willing to represent clients, even if they know that the possibility of winning the case is slim or impossible. Most unfortunately serve these clients because of monetary gain, forgetting or putting aside any moral issues re representing or defending someone who has clearly broken the law or are in the wrong.

The author of books/articles must ensure the initial first few lines or paragraphs attract the prospective reader that their book is worth reading. They must then ensure the entire book's contents are so good and attractive that readers will then recommend the book to others.

Candidates applying for jobs, attending interviews, or sitting for examinations must convince the prospective employer or examiner that they have the suitable qualities and knowledge.

Most photos of celebrities are tampered with to transform the photos into the desired image. Whilst the improved photos encourage the public to aim for better standards to be achieved by themselves, the downside include unrealistic comparisons.

This encourages peer pressure to look like the person's idol and affects the person's judgement re having those expensive and often dangerous beauty treatments.

The above are just some examples of how every person and every profession are salespersons. As a result of having to convince the other party to achieve one's goal, often half-truths are told. The more diplomatic word used in these cases is exaggeration. We will over-exaggerate our strengths and under-exaggerate our weaknesses.

A true salesperson does not sell. They help the person to buy. A true salesperson makes the person aware that there is a solution to the problem they want to resolve.

It is better to be defeated on principle than to win on lies
- Arthur Calwell

All things being equal, people do business with and refer business to those people they know, like and trust.
- Bob Burg

PERSONAL NOTES

Describe a similar situation in your life :

_____

_____

_____

_____

_____

Describe how you may now choose to act differently :

_____

_____

_____

_____

_____

10

YOU LIED?

Let him who is without sin cast the first stone.

Whether we wish to admit this, all humans have lied more than once during their lifetime. There is a clear dividing line between the truth and a lie. When we 'partly' lie, this is called 'half-truth'. Half-truths are also known as White Lies.

Below is Wikipedia's definition of White Lie.

A white lie would cause only relatively minor discord if it were uncovered, and typically offers some benefit to the hearer.

White lies are often used to avoid offence, such as complimenting something one finds unattractive. In this case, the lie is told to avoid the harmful realistic implications of the truth. As a concept, it is largely defined by local custom and cannot be clearly separated from other lies with any authority.

Whilst there are certain crimes committed such as murder which are clearly not acceptable, over the years I have become more tolerant and forgiving towards certain half-truths uncovered.

I wish to share the following Sunday school teaching instilled in my earlier years, from the Bible

John 8:1-11 (New International Version) explains:

[1]But Jesus went to the Mount of Olives.

[2]At dawn he appeared again in the temple courts, where all the people gathered around him, and he sat down to teach them.

[3]The teachers of the law and the Pharisees brought in a woman caught in adultery. They made her stand before the group

[4]and said to Jesus, "Teacher, this woman was caught in the act of adultery.

[5]In the Law Moses commanded us to stone such women. Now what do you say?"

[6]They were using this question as a trap, in order to have a basis for accusing him. But Jesus bent down and started to write on the ground with his finger.

[7]When they kept on questioning him, he straightened up and said to them, "If any one of you is without sin, let him be the first to throw a stone at her."

[8]Again he stooped down and wrote on the ground.

[9]At this, those who heard began to go away one at a time, the older ones first, until only Jesus was left, with the woman still standing there.

[10]Jesus straightened up and asked her, "Woman, where are they? Has no one condemned you?"

[11]"No one, sir," she said. "Then neither do I condemn you," Jesus declared. "Go now and leave your life of sin."

Before the truth can set you free, you need to recognise which lie is holding you hostage.

PERSONAL NOTES

Describe a similar situation in your life :

_____

_____

_____

_____

_____

Describe how you may now choose to act differently :

_____

_____

_____

_____

_____

11

RELIGIOUS PEOPLE & LEADERS

Whilst I do respect religious leaders and persons, over the years, it has also been proven that some such persons are often the worst hypocrites. These persons are often looked up upon. However, their lives as portrayed in public often mask their human weaknesses of sins committed in private.

We have all heard or read of various unbelievable crimes committed by religious persons, ranging from all religions. None of the main religions of the world, Christianity, Catholicism, Buddhism, Hinduism, or Islam have escaped negative publicity where followers have done wrong.

Half-truths are often told by them as well. They preach and encourage us to do what is right or tell the whole truth always but often they do the opposite in their own lives. These people are human as well. We must bear in mind it is difficult being the leader or father figure all the time. Whilst followers and dependants have these persons to look up to and rely on, leaders or father figures do not have anyone.

Below is another Sunday school teaching from The Bible, book of Matthew 7:21-23:

"Not everyone who says to me, 'Lord, Lord,' shall enter the kingdom of heaven, but he who does the will of My Father in heaven. Many will say to me in that day, 'Lord, Lord, have we not prophesied in your name, cast out demons in your name, and done many wonders in your name?' And then I will declare to them, 'I never knew you; depart from me, you who practice lawlessness!"

Even the Bible acknowledges that not all religious leaders and people are what they perceive to be.

For me personally, I have more respect for persons who are not "religious" than those who are "religious" at their convenience only, for example in a House of Worship or by following certain rituals such as fasting but constantly lie and behave differently when they are not in "religious mode!" or when they think no one is observing them.

Society can exist only on the basis that there is some amount of polished lying and that no one says exactly what he thinks. - Lin Yutang

PERSONAL NOTES

Describe a similar situation in your life :

_____

_____

_____

_____

_____

Describe how you may now choose to act differently :

_____

_____

_____

_____

12

CONFESSION BOX

**Man is least himself when he talks in his own person.
Give him a mask, and he will tell you the truth.
-Oscar Wilde**

This best explains why Confession Boxes in churches are private and confidential, where even the priest is unable to see the face of the person making the confession.

It is so much easier confessing your wrongdoings and weaknesses to a stranger or someone we are not so close with. This is because such persons are more likely to accept us as we are and what we have done, rather than our loved ones, who think they know what's best for us and find it harder to accept if we do not live up to their expectations.

Priests in Confession Boxes listening to the confessions of the church members, besides giving them peace of mind through their confessions, can also learn from them too.

Let me quote from a message by Cebu Archbishop Ricardo Cardinal Vidal in the Herald, The Catholic Weekly, February 7th, 2010.

"Learn from the lay people since they have something to share in spiritual and moral matters. The best way a priest can know the condition of God's people is through the confessional. A priest should spend more time in the confessional to know the real needs of the people he serves. We do not know the needs of the people by virtues they exercise; we know their problems by the sins they commit."

Vidal stressed that the clergy must put ahead the needs of the poor before his own, because when a priest opts for himself, the poor always takes the last place. Vidal continues, "The quality of our service is determined by the direction of our desires. If our hearts are directed towards the self, we become masters to be served. When our hearts are directed to God and His people, we become the servants of all."

Perhaps if we are to be more open and not try to dominate how others should live their lives, all of us will be more comfortable in telling the whole truth rather than half-truths.

When it is uncomfortable When it is unpopular Even when it is dangerous to speak the truth, Is the precise time when the truth should be spoken.

I know people who prefer to attend a church which is a distance from where they live to enable their privacy to be maintained from those of their neighbours in the same village/town.

Not everyone has been blessed to have good neighbours. There are many who cannot even trust a neighbour whom they have known and lived on the same street for years to say accept a small parcel or signed for letter delivery on their behalf if they are not at home.

In Western cultures where for example, it is more acceptable for couples to cohabit and have children before marriage. Marriage is a legal document and proof of a couples' commitment towards each other for life. However, is it better for cohabiting couples to tell the whole truth and be condemned by the less accepting Eastern cultures compared to cohabiting couples telling half-truths and living in secret just to please the rest of the world?

**There are only two ways of telling the complete truth–
anonymously and posthumously.
- Thomas Sowell**

Some food for thought!

PERSONAL NOTES

Describe a similar situation in your life :

_____

_____

_____

_____

_____

Describe how you may now choose to act differently :

_____

_____

_____

_____

_____

13

CONGRATULATIONS,
I AM REALLY HAPPY FOR YOU

We have all said this to someone at least once, but have we always meant it?

It is easy to be happy for someone else if their achievement is not something you want or already have and do not mind them achieving the same.

However, would you be telling the whole truth if you were participating in a competition and turned out to be the runner up?

How about if you were always the bridesmaid and never the bride?

Can a woman who is struggling to conceive her first child or unable to have more children really be genuinely telling the whole truth when she congratulates other parents on their pregnancy, birth of their child or children?

Humans are naturally competitive by nature. Parents compare their children's achievements with other children and boast about it amongst themselves. If their children have not done as well, most put more pressure on their children to do better.

Even when someone else has achieved something you already have, you may not be happy, especially if the person has achieved this at a younger age or with less perceived hurdles compared to how old you were or how many hurdles you had to overcome when you achieved it.

Often when someone else achieves the same status, rank or award, our competitive human nature finds it a threat as we are no longer superior to others.

The older generation always compares how much harder things were during their time and tell the younger generation that they have had it much easier. We all get to this stage of comparing at a certain point in our lives. We must remember that with time, things change, and technology has improved our standard of living but also at a cost. We should not just look at one side of the change and forget about the effects of it as well.

Whilst it is good to keep setting higher standards for yourself, you should be happy if someone has achieved something you did not or have something you do not. Many celebrities and successful persons have come from poorer backgrounds and worked hard to be where they are today. They have made lots of sacrifices which are often forgotten by those who just compare. It is very easy to just look at where they are now and what they have achieved, be jealous about it and forget all the hardship and work that has taken place over time.

So, the next time you say to someone 'Congratulations', say it only if you mean it. You do not always have to have the same as someone else. Doctors need nurses, lawyers need clerks, businesspersons need secretaries and homeowners need maids. The list goes on and we all have a role to play in life.

Words may lie but actions will always tell the truth.

PERSONAL NOTES

Describe a similar situation in your life :

_____

_____

_____

_____

_____

Describe how you may now choose to act differently :

_____

_____

_____

_____

_____

14

BEING STRONG AS A LEADER

When faced with a stressful situation as a group/family, there are often one or several persons who must take the lead and remain strong to enable the group a greater chance of succeeding and surviving in that stressful situation.

For example, the family may be going through financial hardship, but the main breadwinner needs to remain positive and encourage the family that things will improve if they all work together. Often times, that main 'leader' may be 'lost for ideas' or even have personal doubts as to how the situation will ever improve but for the sake of maintaining calm within the family, that person needs to maintain a bold and courageous front.

Leaders or even spouses often do not share the whole truth of their emotions to the rest as they do not want to discourage the rest in what is already a very stressful situation.

I do admire Pastors, Assistants and other leaders who are constantly putting the needs of their congregation first. Yes, you may say it is their job, but we need to remember they are also human, who have problems just like the rest of us.

We need to express our gratitude to them more often, even if it is just a simple word of thanks or a thank you note. Have we ever considered how we can help these people instead of always having the "what's in it for me" attitude? Do we pray for our leaders instead of just criticizing them because they are in the limelight and should know better?

It is the same for employees who are constantly only moaning about all the negatives of their job. They need to be thankful and remember all the positives of their job as well.

Have we ever asked our leader "How are you?" and genuinely care, listen, and offer to help, rather than always only expecting care, a listening ear and help from them?

The American Author and Motivational Speaker, Zig Ziglar once encouraged an employee who was unhappy with her job to write and list down everything that she was thankful for. She replied that she could think of none. Zig then asked if she was getting paid for what she does, does she get paid annual leave, bonuses, etc. This lady finally got the message re being thankful for the many things we often take for granted.

Likewise, after a few days, months, years in a relationship, we often take our spouse for granted and concentrate on their negative habits. We need to take time to remember all the positive values that attracted us to that person in the first place.

It is the same for parents. During the younger years, children are often 'cuter and more adorable'. How easy it is for parents to forget how much more they adored their children when they were younger compared to when they become "challenging teenagers" or "irresponsible adults".

Likewise, children are dependent on their parents and elders when they are younger and often forget and despise them once they become more independent.

A truth that is told with bad intent beats all the lies you can invent. - William Blake, "Auguries of Innocence," Poems from the Pickering Manuscript

PERSONAL NOTES

Describe a similar situation in your life :

_____

_____

_____

_____

_____

Describe how you may now choose to act differently :

_____

_____

_____

_____

_____

15

USING THE TRUTH/BELIEF TO SUIT YOUR CIRCUMSTANCES

I have had the privilege of living and working in multicultural societies in various countries. Whilst I do respect everyone's choice of beliefs, it often amazes me that the majority would claim that they are strict followers of certain cultures/ preferences, however, they would often twist the facts/ truth to suit their circumstances.

For example, some people would comment that a dessert is far too sweet even after what seems like they enjoyed it. However, they would add more teaspoonfuls of sugar/ sweetener to their drinks or consume other sugary drinks because they like it, even though it may be a lot sweeter than that dessert they commented about.

Some religions forbid certain foods to be eaten. However, the same persons who claim to follow these religious beliefs strictly would ignore if certain prohibited ingredients were in their favourite snacks and processed foods because they refuse to abstain from their favourite foods.

For example, some vegetarians or vegans who will not eat eggs or butter will still eat ice cream and cake containing eggs and butter. I have come across vegetarians who love cow's cheese but when they are asked to swap to goats' cheese as this is healthier, their response is they cannot stand the smell of products from animals.

It is hard to believe that a man is telling the truth when you know that you would lie if you were in his place.
- Henry Louis Mencken, A Little Book in C Major, 1916

Do Not worry about the haters... They are just angry because the truth you speak, contradicts the lie they live.
- Dr Steve Maraboli

PERSONAL NOTES

Describe a similar situation in your life :

_____

_____

_____

_____

_____

Describe how you may now choose to act differently :

_____

_____

_____

_____

_____

16

LYING TO JUSTIFY YOUR ACTIONS

It is amazing how the Law of Attraction works. Whilst setting myself the goal to complete this book before the end of this year and telling a few friends about it, an ex-colleague voluntarily shared his personal experiences with me, without being aware that I am writing a book about this topic.

He shared how he had many years ago, whilst waiting to board his plane, had totally forgotten about the boarding time as he was busy chatting with his family. He was only aware how late he was when his name was announced during the 'final call' announcement.

When he finally got onto the plane, their stewards and stewardess asked him why he had been so inconsiderate by causing the flight to be delayed. He was too embarrassed to admit the truth so casually replied. "I did my best to arrive at the airport on time but how could I have foreseen that the rented car I was driving would break down?". Without finding out the truth, the stewards and stewardess then had sympathy on him and did not make him feel guilty any further.

Had he told the truth, he would have caused several hundreds of passengers to be very upset with him throughout the flight, which may not have been healthy for everyone concerned.

However, I personally do not agree with the lies he told just to cover up his mistake.

Please do not lie to me, unless you are absolutely certain, I will never find out the truth

PERSONAL NOTES

Describe a similar situation in your life :

_____

_____

_____

_____

_____

Describe how you may now choose to act differently :

_____

_____

_____

_____

_____

17

TALES TOLD BY OLDER FOLKS

My dad used to tell us stories of his youth. One of them was children were told to finish their food and not to leave even a grain of rice in their bowls. The reason given was if they do, they will get a spouse that has "pox marks" on their face. This instilled a fear in children so they will not be wasteful and leave unfinished food in their bowls.

In this case, the half-truths did work during my dad's era and I still hear some parents telling these half-truths to their children to this day.

Another story from my dad was that Chinese families never use any chipped or cracked crockery, as they believe it will bring bad luck. Dad thinks the real reason is that it is not hygienic to use them and so to instil this habit, they put the fear of having bad luck if such crockery is used.

In the West, we often see people not finishing the food on their plates, even when they are guests. They are very honest over their unfinished food, even saying they did not like the taste of the food.

Let us reflect on a typical Chinese meal and a Western meal. In a typical Eastern meal, be it a home cooked meal or on in a restaurant, several dishes are served and laid on the table. In this scenario, the guests can help themselves to the food they like and avoid the ones that they are not too fond of. In this case, there is no wastage and they take what they can consume.

In Western meals, there is no choice as everyone is served the same food, so there may be wastage if the guests do not finish some of the food served to them, be it for whatever reason.

Parents are still telling tales to their children by making them believe that the "Tooth Fairy" or "Santa Claus" exists and it is only when their children grow up that they realise these "fictitious beings" are actually multiple roles played by their parents to encourage their children to be brave for losing their "baby teeth" or to be on good behaviour during the year so that they will be rewarded by gifts during Christmas time.

I am not upset that you lied to me.
I am upset because from now on, I cannot believe you.

PERSONAL NOTES

Describe a similar situation in your life :

_____

_____

_____

_____

_____

Describe how you may now choose to act differently :

_____

_____

_____

_____

_____

18

JUST JOKING VS CREATING TROUBLE

People lie for various reasons. If we reflect and are honest with ourselves, we will be taken aback how often we have lied whether intentionally or unintentionally or even spontaneously.

Sometimes we lie out of fear and sometimes for acceptance. Sometimes we lie to impress on others as well as to boost our ego. These are the occasions when name dropping is done to impress on the audience that you know these people in high places.

My mum is a committee member in her alumni, which is made up of members from all ages and all walks of life, from homemakers, retirees, single parents, and corporate figures. This group likes to joke among themselves pertaining to their status. To an outsider, what is being said should not be taken as the gospel truth.

Recently, a member was asked, "Have you been promoted to GM? (a GM in the business world will mean General Manager). What was asked of her was whether she has become a **g**rand**m**other.

Getting a maid is a big problem in Malaysia so most families are without one. A common question among ladies is, "Do you have a reliable maid?" Many will answer, "Yes", she is on call 24/7. Then this is followed by, "I am the maid!"

My mum attended the City of Coventry Teachers College in Warwickshire in the '60s. As she was the first and only Malaysian in the college, the British students there had a lot of questions to ask her.

One of the questions was, "Do you all live on trees in the jungle, like Tarzan?". My mum has a sense of humour, so in jest she replied, "Yes, we do." She explained that this was because of the wild animals that come out at night. Since we live near riverbanks, it was safer to live on treetops so that we will not be affected by the flood waters. We travel about on rivers in our canoes made from tree trunks or on rafts made from bamboo. Sometimes we tame baby crocodiles and they pull our rafts or canoes for us. My mum said this with a straight face, and she thinks some of them bought her story. One of her lecturers once told her that butter will not melt in my mum's mouth.

Another question was, "Where did you learn how to speak English? "My mum then told them truthfully that it was the missionaries that had set up schools in Malaysia and we were taught by white missionaries from America.

Sometimes people lie to create trouble to others. After my mum retired from teaching, she accompanied my dad to his office daily. One day my dad's secretary passed a phone call to my dad. The caller, a relative from overseas who was in town had asked my dad why he had not contacted her although she had phoned the house and had told my mum she was in town. My parents were taken aback, as it was a big lie as my mum could not be in two places at the same time.

Make yourself an honest man, and then you may be sure there is one less rascal in the world.
- Thomas Carlyle

PERSONAL NOTES

Describe a similar situation in your life :

_____

_____

_____

_____

_____

Describe how you may now choose to act differently :

_____

_____

_____

_____

_____

19

BEING DIPLOMATIC

Often, we must pretend to like or get along with people because they are our friends, suppliers, or clients. If we really had the courage to tell these people how annoying their habits are or what we dislike about them, the relationship will most likely cease and that could affect our jobs or businesses.

In Eastern cultures, children are brought up to respect their elders and often times, even when we feel our elders have hurt us or we do not agree with their decisions or opinions, we have been brought up to remain silent as it is considered disrespectful to argue with elders.

In Western cultures, children are bolder to their elders, even calling parents and elders by their first names, whereas those from Eastern cultures would always refer to elders as Aunty or Uncle and call their parents Mum and Dad.

I once had the unfortunate experience of being present where someone's nineteen year old daughter threw a tantrum and tore up some books that were given to her by her mother because she did not want to face the truth about what was happening to her. The daughter just walked off into her room, leaving us in the dining room. Instead of apologising to us, the guests, for her daughter's rude behaviour, and asking her daughter to come back into the room as my Eastern cultured parents and elders would have done, this Western cultured mother just let her daughter be and instead blamed us for her daughter's behaviour. It took a good six months before this mother came to her senses and apologised for that unfortunate event.

A true relationship is when you can tell each other anything and everything, no secrets, and no lies.

PERSONAL NOTES

Describe a similar situation in your life :

_____

_____

_____

_____

_____

Describe how you may now choose to act differently :

_____

_____

_____

_____

_____

20

WORKING LIFE

It would be a lot simpler if everyone practised the Whole Truth.

For example, when someone cold calls for business.

Some receptionists or the person being cold called, instead of saying they are busy or not interested, they would prefer to tell Half Truths such as "Please call back later". When the person calls again, another delaying tactic excuse is given and only after several attempts does the person tell the Whole Truth or by that time, the cold caller would have given up and moved on. All these Half Truths waste unnecessary time and resources.

Another common lie told by several businesspeople is 'The cheque/item is in the post" or "the job is almost completed". This again wastes a lot of energy and time, which could be avoided when the Whole Truth is practised. If we are unable to pay or manage a deadline, it is always best to be upfront, rather than putting everyone in uncomfortable and inconvenient situations.

Sadly, such bad habits have caused society to be less trusting over time. Some 30 or more years ago, most businesses, even the smaller ones would be more willing to give at least a month's credit before getting paid even for products purchased. These days, because of all the deceit and half-truths, these practices have slowly diminished, and we are now more in a "Pay Upfront" society.

> **Honesty pays, but it does not seem
> to pay enough to suit some people.
> - Frank McKinney "Kin" Hubbard**

> **Honesty saves everyone's time.**

PERSONAL NOTES

Describe a similar situation in your life :

_____

_____

_____

_____

_____

Describe how you may now choose to act differently :

_____

_____

_____

_____

_____

21

MAXIMUM TRUTHS AND MAXIMUM LIES

Maximum Truths have been told in bars with a glass of alcohol in hand. This is because most people go to bars to socialise in a relaxed atmosphere. The alcohol relaxes most drinkers even further and they then let their guards down and share how they really feel.

On the contrary, Maximum lies have been told in Courts, with the Holy Books in hand.

This is because, there will always be a party in Court called The Defendant who is defending oneself from accusations that have resulted in attending Court. The Plaintiff or Accuser on the hand is the one who is bringing a case against the Defendant.

At least one of the parties is in the wrong. However as there is always a penalty or punishment for the person that loses the case, both parties will naturally do their best to win the case, even if half-truths and lies are told.

I swear to Tell the Truth,
the Whole Truth and Nothing but the Truth
so, Help Me God

Truth is Truth, even if no one believes it.
A lie is a lie, even if everyone believes it.

PERSONAL NOTES

Describe a similar situation in your life :

_____

_____

_____

_____

_____

Describe how you may now choose to act differently :

_____

_____

_____

_____

_____

22

MENTORS – Why we need them & how to best benefit from them.

A mentor is someone who has been there and succeeded. They have experience in the area you are looking to progress in. They have previously overcome the challenge you are seeking to solve.

Having a mentor is important as they are upfront on what works and what does not. Mentors will show you how to achieve your goals.

Mentors tell you what you "need" to hear and not what you "want" to hear. To benefit from mentors, you need to run things, however small, by them as you can depend on them not to hold back on The Truth.

It can be uncomfortable for the person being mentored as Whole Truths are being shared about how one is progressing. Often, it means getting out of one's comfort zones and dealing with feedback that may be hard to accept.

A great example is when I was getting ready to publish this book. I sought advice from mentors and friends who have published their own books. I received much appreciated "constructive criticism", the process where valid and well-reasoned opinions about one's work is shared. I received a mixture of positive and negative comments that were shared in a friendly and well-meaning manner.

Constructive criticism should be shared tactfully so that it is easier for the recipient since no one likes receiving negative comments.

A great mentor and friend will never tell you Half Truths as they want you to succeed. They genuinely have your best interests and your goals for growth at heart.

To all my past and present Mentors, this chapter is dedicated to all of you. Thank you for the patience and dedication you have shown in guiding me to where I am today and to all that I will achieve going forward.

Mentoring is a brain to pick, an ear to listen, and a push in the right direction. - John Crosby

PERSONAL NOTES

Describe a similar situation in your life :

_____

_____

_____

_____

_____

Describe how you may now choose to act differently :

_____

_____

_____

_____

_____

23

MOVING ON

Every now and again, we enter a new chapter in our life. We progress from being born, to being a toddler, to being a child, to being a teenager, to being an adult, completing studies, getting a job or starting a business and finally retiring.

The start of each new chapter is often the hardest. It is often the hardest because as humans, we are often comfortable in the existing chapter of our life. It is often hard to move on because the people we may be leaving behind are not ready to move on with us or let go of us.

For those who have been brought up in an Asian Country culture, we are often told to follow customs and traditions. This normally means one must pursue certain professions like being a

Doctor
Accountant
Lawyer or
Engineer

Other careers such as being a musician, artist or chef may be frowned upon.

It is very challenging for children who want to pursue their dreams when parents do not allow or support their chosen careers. This results in internal unhappiness and half-truths being told. Most parents mean well as the world views certain careers as easier paths towards financial freedom.

If you are an independent adult who is unhappy in your current position, I encourage you to make that change, even if it is a tiny step at a time. Share the Whole Truth about what you really want to pursue and pursue it as life is precious and you do not want to leave this world full of regrets.

PERSONAL NOTES

Describe areas in your life you would like to improve :

_____

_____

_____

_____

_____

Describe the steps you are going to take to help you improve :

_____

_____

_____

_____

_____

THIS IS YOUR **LIFE**.

DO WHAT YOU LOVE AND DO IT OFTEN.

IF YOU DON'T LIKE SOMETHING, CHANGE IT. IF YOU DON'T LIKE YOUR JOB, QUIT.

IF YOU DON'T HAVE ENOUGH TIME, STOP WATCHING TV (OR TEXTING)

IF YOU ARE LOOKING FOR THE LOVE OF YOUR LIFE, STOP. THEY WILL BE WAITING FOR YOU WHEN YOU

START DOING THE THINGS YOU LOVE.

STOP OVER ANALYZING.

ALL EMOTIONS ARE BEAUTIFUL.

WHEN YOU EAT, APPRECIATE EVERY LAST BITE.

LIFE IS SIMPLE. OPEN YOUR MIND, ARMS AND HEART TO NEW THINGS AND PEOPLE.

WE ARE UNITED IN OUR DIFFERENCES.

ASK THE NEXT PERSON YOU SEE WHAT THEIR PASSION IS, AND SHARE YOUR INSPIRING DREAM WITH THEM.

TRAVEL OFTEN.

GETTING LOST WILL HELP YOU FIND YOURSELF.

SOME OPPORTUNITIES ONLY COME ONCE, SEIZE THEM.

LIFE IS ABOUT THE PEOPLE YOU MEET, AND THE THINGS YOU CREATE WITH THEM SO GO OUT AND START CREATING.

LIFE IS SHORT.

LIVE YOUR DREAM AND SHARE YOUR PASSION.

- HOLSTEE MANIFESTO

In conclusion, let me leave you with some further quotes to help you decide whether to tell the Whole Truth or Half-Truth in future.

- A half-truth is the most cowardly of lies.

- A half-truth is usually less than half of that

- Beware of the half-truth. You may have gotten hold of the wrong half!

- No man has a good enough memory to make a successful liar. - Abraham Lincoln

- Those who think it is permissible to tell white lies soon grow colour-blind. - Austin O'Malley

- With lies you may get ahead in the world—but you can never go back. - Russian proverb

- When you stretch the truth, watch out for the snapback. - Bill Copeland

- People say they hate lies, but when they are told the truth, they refuse to accept it. - Bishop Bira Fonseca

- When truth is divided, errors multiply. - Eli Siegel, Damned Welcome

- A little inaccuracy sometimes saves tons of explanation. - Saki

- There is one way to find out if a man is honest—ask him. If he says, "Yes," you know he is a crook.
  - Groucho Marx

- I am different from Washington; I have a higher, grander standard of principle. Washington could not lie. I can lie, but I will not. - Mark Twain

- The naked truth is always better than the best dressed lie.

- Political language is designed to make lies sound truthful and murder respectable, and to give an appearance of solidity to pure wind. - George Orwell

- See, in my line of work you got to keep repeating things over and over again for the truth to sink in, to kind of catapult the propaganda. - George W. Bush— 43rd US President

- Who lies for you will lie against you. -Bosnian Proverb

- If you want to ruin the truth, stretch it.

- People prefer delusions because they cannot handle the truth. The truth would require them to deal with the issue.

- People do not want to hear the truth because they do not want their illusions destroyed.

- Whoever is careless with the truth in small matters cannot be trusted with important matters
  - Albert Einstein

- A relationship with no trust is like a car with no fuel. You can stay in it all you want but it will not go anywhere.

- Denying the truth does not change the facts.

- A single lie discovered is enough to create doubt in every truth.

- You cannot walk in the Truth, holding hands with a Lie.
  - Bishop Macedo

- There is nothing wrong with wanting more wealth and success, as long as the journey you choose does not involve you to sacrifice your truth or soul. - Peng Joon

- Stop worrying about what other people think of you. You know the Truth about who you are and that is all that matters.

- Lies are like RUST that will destroy the foundation of every relationship.

- If you think you are rich, there are many who are richer than you. If you think you are clever, there are more people cleverer than you. But if you think you are honest, then you are among the few and in this instance, it is best to be among the few.
  - Tunku Abdul Rahman Putra,
  First Prime Minister of Malaysia

- Sometimes, the best thing you can do is keep your mouth shut & your eyes open. The Truth always comes out in the end.

- Never lie to someone who trusts you, and never trust someone who lies to you.

WHY DO PEOPLE CALL TRUTH, THE NAKED TRUTH?

Simply because the truth is transparent, it has nothing to hide.

There is an amusing Jewish parable that explains how the Truth became the naked Truth.

The story goes that the Truth and the Lie meet one day. The Lie says to the Truth, "It's a marvellous day today". The Truth was suspicious but looks up to the sky and saw that indeed the day was indeed beautiful. They spent a lot of time together, ultimately arriving beside a well.

The Lie then tells the Truth, "The water is very nice, let's take a bath together." The Truth, once again suspicious, tests the water and discovers that it indeed is very nice. They removed their clothes, jumped into the well and started bathing.

Suddenly, the Lie comes out of the well, puts on the clothes of the Truth and runs away. The Truth was startled and also quickly comes out of the well but could not find his clothes. The Truth refused to wear the clothes of The Lie and having nothing to be ashamed of, walked naked in the streets. The naked Truth runs everywhere to find the Lie and to get his clothes back.

The World, seeing the Truth naked, turns its gaze away, with contempt and rage. Since then, the Lie travels around the world, dressed as the Truth, satisfying the needs of society, because the World, in any case, harbours no wish nor desire at all to meet the naked Truth. The World found it easier to accept the Lie dressed as the Truth, than the naked Truth.

This is a remarkable story, but it speaks about what is happening in the world.

The Lie will not always be telling outright lies. The Lie has and will continue to deceive the world with lies, cloaked in Truth.

All truth passes through three stages.
First, it is ridiculed.
Second, it is violently opposed.
Third, it is accepted as being self-evident.
- Arthur Schopenhauer

KEEP YOUR LIFE SIMPLE

Missing somebody ?	CALL
Want to meet up?	INVITE
Want to be understood?	EXPLAIN
Have questions?	ASK
Do not like something?	SAY IT
Like something?	STATE IT
Want something?	ASK FOR IT
Love someone?	TELL THEM

Paying It Forward

If you enjoyed reading this book, I really appreciate your sharing it with others and leaving an honest review online so it may touch other lives.

Thank you and I appreciate every one of you.

Please feel free to connect with me via
calendly.com/wellnessiridology